Robin Klein
Illustrated by Alison Lester

THINGNAPPED!

Melbourne
OXFORD UNIVERSITY PRESS
Oxford Auckland New York

There was a girl at Emily Forbes's school called Stephanie Strobe. She had everything in the world that anyone could possibly want, even her very own ensuite bathroom with a spa pool. She certainly didn't deserve it. Whenever Emily brought anything interesting to school, Stephanie Strobe would look at it, raise her eyebrows under her fringe, open her eyes as wide as hibiscus flowers, and not say anything in a very loud insulting way.

One Friday morning Emily had something special to take to school. Her pet stegosaurus, Thing, had helped capture two burglars, and the Chief Commissioner of Police had sent him a thank you letter. It was sealed with a magnificent blob of red sealing wax. Emily was proud of that letter, but Stephanie Strobe just looked at it as though it were dribble.

'Fancy burglars breaking into *your* place,' she said nastily. 'You'd think they'd realize there was nothing valuable enough to steal.'

Emily linked her hands behind her back, because she knew that if she didn't, she would probably sock Stephanie Strobe. 'Thing's very valuable,' she said. 'I bet he's the only stegosaurus in the whole country, maybe even the whole world.'

Behind her hibiscus eyes, Stephanie Strobe was thinking that someone had something she didn't have! So, when she arrived home from school, she demanded (she didn't ever ask politely for things) that her mother go out and buy *her* a green stegosaurus.

'I don't think you can buy them at any of the local shops,' her mother said nervously, for Stephanie had the most awful temper if she didn't get her own way immediately. 'Would it do if I bought you a Great Dane puppy instead?'

Stephanie threw herself down on the floor and bellowed like a buffalo. 'I want a green stegosaurus like Emily Forbes!' she roared, biting a chunk out of the piano. 'It's not fair! You'll just have to find a shop that does sell them! Right now! This minute!'

So Mrs Strobe had to get out the car and drive around in peak hour traffic. She couldn't find a local shop that sold stegosauruses, and was too scared to face Stephanie empty-handed, so she bought a very expensive Stephanie-sized white fur jacket.

Stephanie threw it up on the roof in a rage because it wasn't a stegosaurus.

'I'll go into the city tomorrow and look,' her mother promised hastily.

Stephanie made sure she did, by nagging and bullying and being so unpleasant that Mrs Strobe left very early on Saturday morning.

Stephanie hung over the front gate waiting impatiently for her to come back. She saw Emily Forbes taking Thing into the park opposite to play. Suddenly she couldn't bear to wait for her mother to come back from the city with a stegosaurus.

Stephanie crossed the street to the park and hid behind a bench.

Emily and Thing were playing hide and seek. Thing put his paws over his eyes. He couldn't count past ten, but knew that hide and seek needed much more than that, so he counted up to ten five times. Then he went looking for Emily. She had found a good place to hide, in the fork of a willow tree. Thing knew she was there. He could see her shoe dangling, but pretended he didn't. He went all around the park, even turning over small pebbles to look underneath, and peering up in to the park tap. And when the willow tree was the last place left, he pretended to be amazed to find Emily there.

Then it was Emily's turn to count. She shut her eyes and put her hands over her ears, too. Thing was apt to get excited when it was his turn to hide, and forgot about the noise his feet made pounding from one place to another. Emily always counted up to three hundred and fifty, because it was only fair. There was more of Thing to be hidden.

'One, two, three,' she began to count. Thing galloped past the bench where Stephanie was hiding. His favourite hiding place was the park litter bin. He couldn't fit into it, of course, but he put it over his head like a helmet. Because it turned the world black and he couldn't see, he always thought Emily couldn't see him, either. So he sat there happily with his head in the litter bin, and waited for Emily to come and find him.

Stephanie Strobe crept out from behind the bench and snatched the litter bin away. Thing blinked. He'd expected Emily, but wagged his tail, thinking that Stephanie just wanted to join in the game of hide and seek, too.

'I know a much better place to hide,' she whispered craftily. 'Emily will think you're very clever if you hide in the lovely place I show you.' She steered Thing towards the gate, and he went willingly. He thought she was kind and generous to show him a new hiding place.

Stephanie hurried him through the park gate and across the street to her house, which was almost as splendid as the Taj Mahal. There was a vast entrance hall paved with black and white tiles, and a staircase curving far above Thing's head. 'Upstairs,' Stephanie ordered, and gave him a push. Thing obediently climbed the stairs. A door leading into the kitchen opened and Mrs Strobe looked out.

Thing froze. Emily had trained him to freeze into various disguises in an emergency, so he made himself look like a large green candelabra. He didn't seem out of place on that rich staircase, which was already crammed with marble figures, big pots of ferns on pedestals, and stained-glass windows.

'I drove and walked all through town, but I still couldn't find a shop that sold stegosauruses,' Mrs Strobe said apologetically. 'Do you want me to go to the market tomorrow and try there?'

'Yes!' snapped Stephanie. She didn't want anyone to know about Thing just yet, in case she was made to give him back.

'I've heated some vegetable soup for lunch,' said Mrs Strobe.

'I want lemon meringue pie instead!' Stephanie yelled, kicking a big brass pot down the stairs. Her mother jumped back into the safety of the kitchen and shut the door. Thing waited to be told that it was all right to unfreeze, but Stephanie said crossly, 'Why are you lying around with your feet stuck up in the air? Hurry up and get upstairs!'

She opened the door of her room and pushed him inside. Stephanie's room was enormous. It had to be, to hold Stephanie's many thousands of possessions that she'd bullied her parents into buying. Her bed was magnificent enough to have belonged to King Henry the Eighth or Cleopatra, and was strewn with opened boxes of chocolates. Stephanie was so greedy and spoiled that she just bit once into each separate chocolate, for she knew that there were plenty more where they came from.

On the bedside table was a cassette recorder. Stephanie liked to listen to the sound of her own voice, and also to make lists of more things she wanted if she woke during the night. The bedroom walls were covered with scribbled messages, most of them starting with I HATE, such as I HATE EMILY FORBES, and I HATE NOT GETTING MY OWN WAY.

Stephanie didn't give Thing time to look properly at that room. She shoved him into her ensuite bathroom and threw the smallest box of chocolates in after him. Then she slammed the door, locked it and yelled through the keyhole: 'You can just forget about Emily Forbes! She doesn't want you any more because you're so boring; she told me so at school yesterday. She said I could have you now. You'll have to live there in the bathroom, because I don't want you messing around in my room. Those chocolates are for your lunch and dinner. You can't expect me to waste my time cooking special meals and bringing them up on a tray. *Wheeeee!* Now I've got a stegosaurus and Emily Forbes hasn't!'

And she rushed downstairs to make sure her mother put plenty of meringue on the lemon pie.

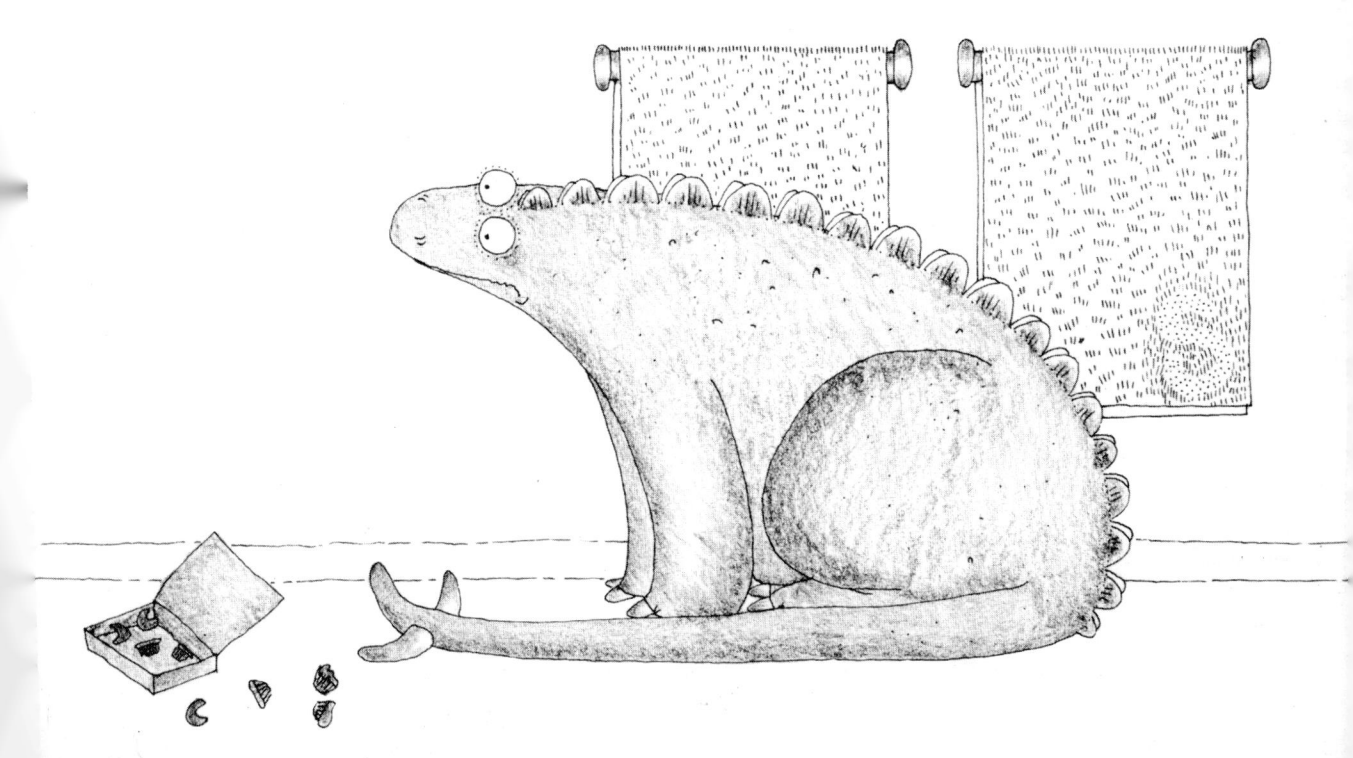

Emily hunted through the park until the afternoon sun cast long shadows, growing more and more worried. Then she went home, hoping desperately that Thing might have gone there, though he hadn't ever done so without waiting for her. But the flat was empty. Thing wasn't in the living room watching television. He wasn't in the shower recess playing Superman in a phone box. He wasn't sitting patiently in front of the refrigerator waiting for someone to open the door so he could have a banana. He wasn't visiting Mrs McIlvray in the downstairs flat.

The table was set for dinner, with Thing's new table decoration as a centrepiece, just as they'd left it before going to the park to play. His favourite TV show at the moment was one called *Make Stunning Table Decorations and Surprise All Your Friends*. Emily and her mother were surprised and stunned every night. Thing made very original centrepieces. The one on the table now was an old plastic rainhat of Emily's filled with modelling clay, with three toffee apples stuck in it. Emily looked at it and burst into tears.

When her mother, who was a taxi driver, came home from work and heard that Thing was missing, they drove all around the streets near the park. They even went back to the oval where Emily had found him in a Vegemite-coloured stone egg, and to the shopping centre carpark where she took him skateboarding. But he wasn't in any of those places.

'Try not to worry, Emily,' Mrs Forbes said, trying to hide her own anxiety. 'Thing won't have gone very far. He's too chubby for long hikes. I'm sure he'll be back tomorrow.'

'Dozens of awful things could have happened to him,' Emily said miserably. 'He could have fallen into a river. I don't think he can swim, either. When we went to the pool, and I was going to teach him, the manager wouldn't let us in.'

'I think he could swim if he had to,' Mrs Forbes said gently. 'Think of all the sports programmes he watches on TV. He's sure to have picked up the general idea of swimming from them. All we can do is go home and wait.'

Mrs McIlvray was just as concerned as they were. She made a bowl of Thing's favourite salad and put it outside her door, in case he came home during the night. Then she went to bed, but she had just the same amount of sleep as Emily and Mrs Forbes. None at all.

Thing heard what Stephanie Strobe said, but the words were so terrible he didn't let them stay inside his mind. He just knew that Emily was counting up to three hundred and fifty and hadn't reached the end yet. He ate two of the chocolates, even though Stephanie had bitten a half moon in each one while trying to find a strawberry soft centre. The chocolates weren't nearly as nice as the salads made by Mrs McIlvray. They made him feel sick, so he went for a walk around Stephanie's enormous bathroom and looked at the spa pool.

Thing had seen spa pools advertised on television, and thought he'd try this one while waiting for Emily. He climbed in and turned on the little jets of bubbling water. He played a rather lonely game of boats with the little fluted paper cups that held the chocolates. Emily was taking such a long time to come and find him that he fell asleep among all the bubbles.

Next morning Mrs Strobe brought Stephanie breakfast in bed — ice cream with hundreds and thousands, because Stephanie always threw a tantrum if she had to eat porridge and toast like everyone else.

'I don't want you tidying up my room any more,' Stephanie said. 'I like it messy. You're not to go in my bathroom, either. I've turned it into a laboratory. I've fixed it so a bomb will explode if you go in there.'

Mrs Strobe believed her, for she knew very well what Stephanie was like. She gave up her usual Sunday golf and drove to all the weekend markets to find Stephanie a green stegosaurus. Stephanie finished her ice cream breakfast, forgetting to give Thing any breakfast at all, and went off to play.

Thing spent a long, uneasy day in the spa pool, waiting for Emily. Sometimes he got out and went for a walk around Stephanie's bathroom, and weighed himself on her scales. It was something to do while waiting, but it was just as well he couldn't read the dial on the scales.
For Thing was shrinking.
Rapidly.
The combination of nothing to eat and spa pool bathing was having a drastic effect on his figure. He did notice that each time he got back into the pool, the taps seemed higher, but everything was so upsetting and strange about Stephanie's house that one more odd thing wasn't remarkable. He became so desperately hungry that he took the lid from a jar of cold cream, thinking it might be vanilla yoghurt, but it tasted awful. So he slipped back into the pool, wondering why the sides were becoming so steep, and why Emily was taking so long to find him.

For Stephanie, the best part of owning Thing was going to school the next day and seeing how sad and quiet Emily Forbes looked. And after school she followed Emily secretly to see what she would do. Emily went to the park. She'd gone there many times since Thing was missing; it was the only place she could think of to look for him. She stood in the counting place and counted slowly to three hundred and fifty. She was hoping that when she reached the end of the counting, Thing would be sitting miraculously on the grass with the litter bin over his head. But that didn't happen.

'Lost something?' Stephanie called out, smirking, and skipped across the street to her house. Her mother wasn't home. There was a note on the hall table. 'Stephanie, as none of the markets had green stegosauruses, I'll spend today driving around the suburbs to check all the shopping centres. Please don't be cross at the delay. Love and apologies, Mother.'

Stephanie scarcely bothered to read the note, and didn't notice how tired and worn out the handwriting looked. She was too busy checking to make sure that her mother had prepared a delicious afternoon tea for her before going out. She ate it greedily, saving only half a scone which she took upstairs. She opened the bathroom door a crack.

Thing, who'd been smelling her frangipanni talcum powder, hoping that it was edible, hastily put the lid back on and crept under the bathmat. He was scared of Stephanie now, and very glad that she didn't come right into the room.

'Leave my talcum powder alone, you stupid green thing!' she said sharply. 'I never share my things with anyone! I've got a message from Emily Forbes for you.'

Thing ran forward joyfully, getting tangled with the bathmat fringe in his excitement.

'Emily said to tell you that she's delighted that you aren't living at her place any more. She's going to the Lost Dogs' Home to get a new pet. She said she's always wanted a dog instead of a stegosaurus, so you'd better be grateful that I've taken you in and given you a home. It's certainly a whole lot bigger and richer than Emily Forbes's poky little flat.'

Those hideous words mingled with the other terrible ones she'd already tossed at Thing. He fought a tremendous battle and pushed both lots out of his mind. Stephanie seemed to have grown much taller, larger and noisier, and he couldn't understand why. Her eyes, when she looked down at him, weren't friendly and sparkling like Emily's.

'You've shrunk and lost weight,' Stephanie said critically. 'That's convenient. Emily Forbes wouldn't even recognize you now. If I took you out on a leash, she'd just walk straight by. You've got to learn a lot of tricks now that you belong to me, like jumping through a fire hoop while balancing a ball on your nose. When you can do that, I'll open a circus and make a lot of money, even more than I have already. That's all you're good for, anyhow, being in a circus. You'll have to walk along a tightrope a hundred metres up in the air. I could even advertise you as the smallest stegosaurus in the world, if you lost enough weight. And the quickest way to make that happen is not to feed you anything at all!'

She popped the half scone into her own mouth, and for the next three days she didn't bother to come near him at all, or bring him anything to eat, not even a chewed chocolate.

During those three days, Mrs Strobe wore herself out searching every shop in every suburban shopping centre. When she was home in between doing that, she dodged Stephanie because she was too scared to say that she still hadn't found a stegosaurus. On Friday, with Stephanie safely at school, she looked around at the neglected house and thought that she really must tidy it before going out to search through even more distant shopping centres.

She opened the front door to air the house, then collected all her cleaning equipment and went upstairs. In spite of the bomb, she felt she should tidy Stephanie's bedroom and bathroom. She attended to the mess in Stephanie's bedroom, then nervously opened the bathroom door. No bomb exploded, so she went in.

At first she didn't see Thing. He'd shrunk right down to the size of a cabbage from hunger and too many spa baths, and was huddled under the bathmat, wondering uneasily why Emily had sent a lady giant to find him instead of coming herself. Mrs Strobe polished the bathroom basin and wiped up some spilled talcum powder. Then she picked up the bathmat and shook it.

Then she saw Thing.

Even though he'd shrunk to the size of a cabbage, Thing still looked rather startling to strangers. You certainly don't expect to find a small green stegosaurus crouched under a bathmat which you have picked up to shake. Mrs Strobe jumped up on the edge of the bath and yelled.

Thing got such a fright he scuttled through the open door, through Stephanie's bedroom and along the passage till he came to the staircase. There was a steep and enormous drop in between each step, not at all as he'd remembered. But Thing knew that down those changeable stairs there was a front door, and opposite that front door, with just the width of a street between, was a park. And in the park there would be Emily.

He slithered from one step to another all the way to the bottom. He charged across the black and white tiles, each one nearly as big as a bathmat now that he'd shrunk, and out through the door and the front gate. He stared across at the park.

Whenever he'd crossed that street with Emily, it had taken only four or five happy bounds, checking carefully to make sure that no cars were coming. But something had happened to that street since he'd last seen it. Now the park seemed almost as far away as a horizon, and the immense distance in between was filled with towering traffic that roared above his head. Thing knew he'd never be able to cross safely by himself. It had taken dozens of tiny footsteps just to get from Stephanie Strobe's front gate to the kerb. Footsteps as small as that were no match against such frightening traffic.

He sat down on the kerb and looked wistfully across at the park.

After a while an enormous person came up beside him and set down a shopping basket while waiting for a break in the traffic. Thing quickly scrambled up the basket's white wicker side and tumbled down into some Friday afternoon messages. The owner picked up the basket and stepped off the kerb. Thing was carried safely across the street with a jacket going to the drycleaner's, some letters going to be posted and a cracked lampshade being returned to the hardware store to be complained about. He was worried that he might be carried past the park entrance, so he scaled the lampshade and ran along the basket handle till he came to some fingers. He very politely nudged the fingers.

An earthquake happened to the basket and Thing fell off. The basket owner was making such a fuss that several people stopped to ask her what was wrong. 'A horrid little green cabbage thing, right there on my basket handle!' she cried. 'It had spikes along its back and it smelled of frangipanni talcum powder!'

Thing froze, looking so much like a discarded, scrunched-up green plastic bag that the people stopped searching the ground curiously and went away. Thing went away, too, hurrying as fast as he could into the park.

After school that day, Stephanie Strobe followed Emily again, just to gloat. 'Still going into the park to look for that stupid stegosaurus, Emily Forbes?' she jeered. 'I wouldn't bother. Obviously he's found some place to stay that he likes much better than your old flat. Why don't you give up? You're never going to find him now.'

Emily looked at the park in its winter framework of bare trees. Small birds perched on the empty branches, and they seemed to Emily like little black notes on a stave of music, composing a sad song. Thing wasn't in the park. He'd never be there again, waiting for her to find him. It was useless, just as Stephanie Strobe had said.

'My mother's buying *me* a stegosaurus,' Stephanie said. 'She's been looking through all the shops, and she's bound to find one today. I asked her to get a tiny one, so you can't accuse me of kidnapping yours. I expect you'll feel very upset when you see me walking around with my little green stegosaurus on a leash tomorrow!'

And she strutted home, very pleased with herself.

'I want cherry chocolate cake for dinner tonight,' she said to her mother, without even saying hello first.

'I'm not going to make cherry chocolate cake for dinner, tonight or any other night!' said her mother fiercely. Stephanie stared at her in surprise.

'How dare you make me drive all over town and through markets and over every shopping centre in every suburb all week!' Mrs Strobe yelled. 'And now I find out that you've had a green stegosaurus hidden in your ensuite bathroom! Your *ex* ensuite bathroom, I should say! You certainly don't deserve one, so I'm turning it into a nice little study, for my use only, and if you ever dare put a foot inside it, something much worse than a bomb will happen to you!'

Stephanie threw herself down to have a tantrum, but her mother just stepped over her as though she were a draught stopper. 'Even that stegosaurus didn't like you,' she said crushingly, on her way upstairs to her new private study. 'I'm not surprised he ran away.'

So Stephanie had to have the tantrum all by herself without an audience, and developed acute laryngitis. The laryngitis lasted two weeks. And by the end of that time, Mrs Strobe had grown so fond of peace and quiet that she made it quite clear that she wasn't going to put up with any tantrums ever again.

Emily walked slowly across the park when Stephanie left. She stood in the counting place to say goodbye to the memory of Thing. And when that was over, she thought sadly, she'd go home and tell Mrs McIlvray not to put a bowl of salad out on the front step any more at night. After that, she'd pack away all Thing's possessions, the car inner tyre that was his bed, the toffee-apple table decoration, the origami taxi he'd made in honour of Mrs Forbes's birthday, the football boot he'd found one day on the oval. Thing hadn't minded that it wasn't four boots. He would put it on each night to watch TV, letting each of his feet have a turn, and pretend he was a famous footballer.

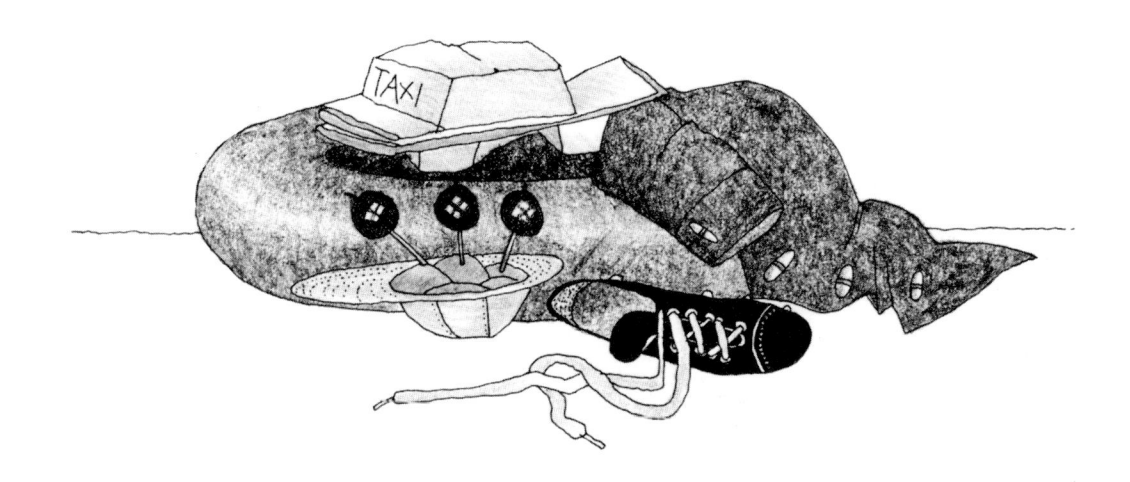

Emily stood quite still in the counting place and put her hands over her ears and shut her eyes. She counted slowly up to three hundred and fifty. Each number was just a way of putting off the time when she would have to walk out of the park and not think about Thing ever again. But even though she counted as slowly as possible, there came the dreadful moment when she had to open her eyes and turn away and walk towards the park gate.

The litter bin was lying on its side, and she bent and picked it up, reminding herself fiercely that she mustn't think about it having been Thing's favourite hiding place.

Someone, she noticed, had put a cabbage in the bin. A rather odd cabbage, with spikes. Emily stared down at it, and as she stared, she saw that it had four little green feet as well as spikes. Thing unfroze from being a cabbage, stretched out to his full length (what there was left of it now) and tried to do something about licking away all the mysterious tears that were spilling down Emily's face. She'd never cried before when she found him in a game of hide and seek!

He certainly didn't have peanut butter sandwiches for his dinner, like Stephanie Strobe. When he reached his third helping of the delicious salad Mrs McIlvray, Mrs Forbes and Emily made for him, they could see him starting to grow under their eyes.

'He certainly has lost a lot of weight,' said Mrs McIlvray. 'But we'll soon take care of that.'

'I wonder where he's been all this time,' said Mrs Forbes. 'As well as being so small, he smells of frangipanni talcum powder!'

Emily didn't say anything, because she was so happy to have him back. Neither did Thing. He curled up in his tyre, wondering sleepily why Emily had taken so long to count to three hundred and fifty.

OXFORD UNIVERSITY PRESS AUSTRALIA

Oxford New York Toronto
Delhi Bombay Calcutta Madras Karachi
Petaling Jaya Singapore Hong Kong Tokyo
Nairobi Dar es Salaam Cape Town
Melbourne Auckland
and associated companies in
Berlin Ibadan

OXFORD is a trademark of Oxford University Press

This book is copyright. Apart from any fair dealing for the purposes of private study, research, criticism or review as permitted under the Copyright Act, no part may be reproduced by any process without written permission. Inquiries should be made to the publishers.

© Text Robin Klein 1984
© Illustrations Alison Lester 1984

First published 1984
Reprinted 1985 twice, 1986
Reprinted in this edition 1986, 1988

NATIONAL LIBRARY OF AUSTRALIA CATALOGUING IN PUBLICATION DATA

Klein, Robin,
  Thingnapped!

  For children.
  ISBN 0 19 554784 5

  I. Lester, Alison. II. Title.

A823'.3

TYPESET BY BOOKSET, MELBOURNE
PRINTED IN AUSTRALIA BY IMPACT PRINTING
PUBLISHED BY OXFORD UNIVERSITY PRESS, 253 NORMANBY ROAD, SOUTH MELBOURNE